FROM YOUTH
— TO —
OLD AGE

•••

A Love Journey of Forever Endurance

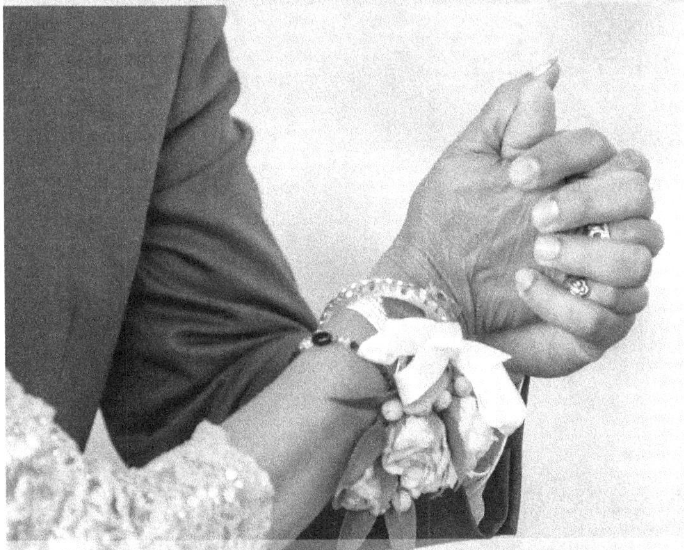

DR. STANLAUS D. LUWANDA, MD

First Edition: August, 2024
Copyright © 2024

Dr. Stanlaus Luwanda, MD
+255 786 334 448, stanlaus@outlook.com
www.stanthechange.mailerpage.io
Musoma, Tanzania

Edited by Daudi Lubeleje
+255 764 771 298, appointments@daudipages.com
www.daudipages.mailerpage.io
Arusha, Tanzania

Typesetting & cover design
DL Bookstore
+255 787 163 013
authors@dlbookstore.com
www.dlbookstore.com
Arusha, Tanzania

ISBN 978-9912-42-091-5

Contents

Dedication

This book is dedicated to:

My family and my wife, Dr. Marina Martin, who is my God-chosen partner and the only one in my life. This book holds significant meaning for our journey together as we grow in our marriage into old age.

To all married and unmarried individuals who aspire to cultivate a positive and nurturing relationship and family, from youth to old age, this book will work wonders in your life.

Your relationship, your marriage, your covenant, your determination, your dreams, your family, and your children are the values you must protect and nurture—not only in your youth but throughout your entire life. The time to start is right here and now!

May the Lord, God, be with you.

"Happy are those who read, learn from one another, and find positive ways to overcome their differences as they grow together in marriage."

— Dr. Stanlaus Luwanda, MD

Appreciation

Love comes from God; through Him, all relationships and marriages are strengthened and blessed with enduring happiness.

I would like to give thanks to the Lord, God, for the strength, protection, and wisdom He has bestowed upon me. Without His guidance, this work would not exist to help strengthen and nurture your relationship.

I would also like to extend my deepest gratitude to my beautiful wife and dear friend, Dr. Marina Martin, for her insightful reviews, the quality time we share, the daily lessons, motivation, and unwavering support in my endeavors. May God bless you abundantly in our life together.

To my parents, Mr. & Mrs. Oscar Dimosso: Your marriage has taught me invaluable lessons about how a positive and inspiring union should be.

My father's love has shaped my positive outlook on marriage and love, and these lessons will be passed down from generation to generation. My mother's reminders have transformed my dreams into reality. You are both a blessing from God, and I will always cherish you in my life.

I am also grateful to everyone who has supported my deep reflections on the protection of love and marriage.

Lastly, my thanks go to DL Bookstore for your tremendous support in reviewing, layout design, and cover design. Your dedication to my work is truly appreciated.

If you were to date again, would you choose your current partner?

You need Positive Inspirational Endurance in your marriage. You need to:

E – *Explore each other,*

N – *Nourish your love,*

D – *Discipline each other,*

U – *Understand each other's needs,*

R – *Respect one another,*

A – *Accept each other's strengths and weaknesses,*

N – *Naturalize your relationship,*

C – *Care for and comfort each other in marriage,*

E – *Enjoy your lifelong partnership.*

Remember to walk this path daily in your relationship.

Introduction

"A new command I give you, Love one another. As I have loved you, so you must love one another. By this everyone will know that you are my disciples, if you love one another." **John 13:34-35.**

Love is the key. Love is a gift. Love is patience. Love is everything you can achieve and live by in this life. Remember to love one another with all your heart. Let your love endure from youth to old age. Love requires commitment. It touches every action and deed of your daily life.

Have you ever been in a romantic relationship? Is your goal to get married in the future? Love is a pathway that always lives among us. Cherish the love you create day by day—these efforts will shape your future.

Cultivating and nurturing love is not a one-time event but a daily practice. Success begins with love in everything you do. Once in love, build peace and happiness. Let love be the foundation of your work, just as it is in your business, studies, leadership, and other key areas of your life. This is the most important work of all. It doesn't require money, but it does demand daily commitment.

Lovers have many expectations and dreams. You are no stranger to this. For decades, it has been the same. We witness people getting married, divorced, breaking up, committing suicide, cheating, and more. These things happen and will continue to happen in the future. Everyone talks about love—some find the motivation to build strong relationships, while others do not. This is our world, full of conflicts, more courtship issues, parenting challenges, and an increasing number of single mothers in a rapidly changing economy. All these problems need solutions. Where is **LOVE?**

There are many circumstances in life that can break your heart when it comes to love. Some of the most important and influential people in your life may not inspire you at all with how they live. Every day may seem like a mess—fathers who do not care for their children, mothers who abandon them. Children growing up without the guidance of their biological parents, left to teach themselves. In the end, they grow up without understanding what love truly means. How will they learn to love you? How will they grasp the meaning of the word *"love"*? What happens if that child is destined to love your son or becomes the person you marry?

Love needs to be learned

Time moves on, waiting for no one. Today you are a child, but tomorrow you will be an old man, telling your history and sharing stories. Many people will listen and learn from you. They will expect much from you. Your life, your actions, and your words will shape what they learn. How do you live your life? Will it be inspirational, or will it extinguish the hopes of the next generation? Ask yourself these questions every day. This world is not yours alone—it is a world we share together. We need companionship, but we also need a life filled with love. Your face is recognized by those close to you. Always remember that.

You are an adult now, and your mind is contemplating starting a relationship. This is your time. You are exposed to many facets of life, and your body may urge you to find a love partner. Sometimes, there may be pressure from friends and those around you. Peer pressure can have a significant impact on your life—sometimes positive, but sometimes detrimental. Despite the circumstances, you manage to begin a fresh and first love relationship. You are no longer alone. Your love journey has begun. But how long will this journey last? Is it forever? What does "forever" mean? Think about that! Don't hesitate if you are ready to move forward in love. Be prepared to fulfill your responsibilities.

This is love—a journey from youth to old age. Aim for that. Do not take it lightly. It is going to be your new place to work, invest, and celebrate your efforts. Love is a partnership between two people willing to move forward together and learn from each other. If you are new to love, be ready to learn and understand. Quarrels, boring moments, and misunderstandings will happen. These are the moments that build your strength and courage to repair your love boat. Never allow your love boat to veer off course or sink before completing your journey together. Listen, and you will understand.

Welcome to the journey. Learn and gain more lessons about relationships and marriage. Learn to motivate, encourage, and restore hope in your partner. Let your love be filled with hope, faith, and happiness. Don't forget to put God at the center of your love. Love without God's grace is like a boat floating, hoping for a wind to determine its direction and course. Once the wind stops blowing, you won't know where you are going. This is love—a journey of committed partners who are willing to live together until old age.

Are you ready for change?

Now, embark on the journey as you prepare to read and learn through your love life. Don't lose your way because your love needs to last from youth to old age.

Love in the Beginning

Sweet words always bring comfort to the one you love. Once in love, you naturally develop beautiful and sweet language to use. There's no secret to it—words come automatically. This is to please your partner and fulfill your desires from him or her.

Love is a language that can be used to communicate and express your feelings. It can be shown through words or actions, and both are equally meaningful as long as your partner understands. Some people are very good at speaking, while others are not. It's a skill that everyone develops over time. Words have the power to convey your desires, emotions, and more. Simple and kind words, when communicated lovingly, are very powerful.

The tone of your words is crucial—it should reflect love. Sometimes, a person may feel comforted just by your voice and tone, even forgetting what you were saying.

Words hold great power in love. When words, voice, and tone are combined, they form a perfect net to catch your "fish." When approaching someone you love, always use kind words. Even if she reject you today, continued exposure to your words, tone, and voice might change her mind. Use this power for good; do not use your skills to manipulate people. You've been given the power to make someone love you, so use it wisely. Some people can make more than one person fall for them because of their skillful use of words. These are the *"masters of words"*—once they speak, the prey is caught.

Your actions define you. You may have sweet and calm words, but if your actions speak differently, they can have a stronger influence. People often observe your actions and follow your lead without you knowing. How do you manage your actions when approaching a woman or when someone approaches you? Are your intentions positive and genuine? A person might reject something, but his or her actions could show a high level of acceptance. This is because actions often speak louder than words. Be mindful of your actions, especially when they might convey a different message to the person you love.

The person you love will start learning new things from you. They will notice your actions—how you do things, how you talk, how you present yourself, and more. These actions speak volumes. If they please your partner, consider yourself lucky. It takes time, so be patient while they keep learning. Love starts with learning and grows through learning. Be sincere in this new journey of love. Do not fake it—your actions should be genuine.

Be Ready to Begin Your Love Journey

Love is a gift. Be ready to receive and cherish it within your heart. Before you start a relationship, ask yourself these questions and make sure you have positive answers before moving forward:

- What kind of relationship do you want at the beginning?

- What is your goal in this love? Will you be satisfied?

- What are your intentions, dreams, and plans? Do you plan to move forward together in everything?

- What if the person you are interested in is different from what you expected? Will this make you lose hope?

- What happens after you fall in love? What's next? Is the journey over?

- Are you ready for this love journey?

Love raises many questions, especially when it comes to accepting another person into your life. When you were alone, you had your own preferences. But now, you need someone to share your life with. She or he might match your expectations, but over time, you will discover his or her true self. Love needs time together, where you teach each other and get to know the person better. It's during this time that your questions will be answered with real-life experiences. If they were good, they will likely continue to be as you thought. You need time for that!

Adulthood is when most relationships begin. This is due to the sexual development that occurs in both males and females, creating a desire for a sexual partner of the opposite sex. This is an important stage where you start learning about love and the kind of love you want in your life. During this period, emotions take control of your body, and you feel the need for a partner. However, you might not be fully prepared for it. Every adolescent you meet seems to talk about love, and it becomes a main focus at this age until you find something that satisfies your body and mind.

Use this time of adulthood to learn what love, sex, and relationships truly mean. Seek knowledge about love and how people perceive it. Use this understanding to see if it fits your life. Sometimes people say *"love,"* but its meaning varies from person to person. Be ready to learn and understand what love means to you. This is the time to prepare for your future life. Build strength and courage. You might not have a loving partner now, but be patient while learning the true meaning of LOVE in your life. This will help you greatly. While others rush into relationships, remain calm and focus on gaining knowledge and preparing for the kind of love you want to build in your future.

You need to be ready. Love will not wait for you—it often comes when you least expect it. Think about why you want to be in a relationship now. Consider the benefits you seek and the potential consequences at your age.

Your fears, peer pressure, emotions, and the advice of your elders should guide your thinking about love. However, they should not completely dictate what you do with your life. Be the main controller of your thoughts and decisions concerning love. Never allow someone to make 100% of your decisions for you. Use your mind to evaluate what you've learned from others and think carefully before acting. Believe in yourself!

When you are ready for love, it's time to begin—not to try.

How Do You Know You're Ready?

Love is strange. It's often amusing to remember how you started your relationship. In the beginning, you might have refused every approach made toward you. It might have been extremely difficult for someone to convince you about entering a relationship. You were strong in your resolve. But later on, you find yourself loving, caring, and happy in that relationship. That's the power of love.

There are no set rules for recognizing when you're ready for love. We all perceive and experience the word *"love"* differently. What works perfectly for one person may not apply to another. It's important to acknowledge that. That's why we say, "no one is perfect." What is perfect for you may be different for someone else.

Use this idea when approaching a woman you like. It's like teaching her what you need from her. Love involves teaching each other every day.

Consider these questions to evaluate whether you're ready for a relationship. They are tips, not rules. Take some time, grab a pen and paper, and list what you know about love in a relationship. Keep this list private, away from others' eyes. Be cautious with friends—they might laugh at you if they find out, and you could lose confidence in exploring your inner self. Also, ask yourself questions about your readiness for love. Remember to tick what aligns with your choices. Check this out:

• Are you old enough to have a partner in love?. Categorize your age according to years in relation to your expected love partner. This is important to know who you are going to date and what his or her likely needs will be. Put a tick to your age group.

Your age group	Male	Female
15 – 19	☐	☐
20 – 24	☐	☐
25 – 30	☐	☐
31 – 35	☐	☐
More than 35	☐	☐

• What happens if you meet him or her? Will you be able to talk freely like you do when you're alone? Is that too tough to think about?. If it's tough, then by how much? What is your way forward?

• What is meant by love? Are you ready for it?

• Are you able to provide for her?. Conduct an assessment of your finances. Evaluate your income to determine if you're in a position to begin a relationship. This is crucial when it comes to providing in love. You'll need money for travel, housing, gifts, phone calls, paying dowry, and other expenses. Assess your situation—whether mild, moderate, severe, or life-threatening. Don't underestimate this. Love without a stable financial foundation invites trouble. It can undermine your confidence and self-worth.

• What are the beliefs and customs of the one you love? Are you ready to learn and nurture them? Understanding and respecting your partner's customs and beliefs is vital. To avoid trauma, misunderstandings, conflicts, and rejection, assess these key issues. If your partner holds their customs and beliefs dearly, be careful not to challenge or undermine him or her because of your love. Respect his or her priorities and consider if you can align with them on this journey.

This is my short list. You can create your own to gauge your readiness for love. Try it at least three times in different seasons. Compare your answers to identify what concerns you most when it comes to love in a relationship. This process will give you hope and courage, reinforcing the idea that anything is possible when you put thought into it. Don't rely solely on this short list. Explore other ways to assess your readiness for love.

Be creative in your life. Know your age, your limits, and your current interests. Let love not disrupt your current lifestyle. You need to know yourself first before falling in love. Your age, work status, or income doesn't matter. If you feel ready to fall in love, then let it happen. Be happy and love with all your heart. Enter with peace and live with peace. A relationship is a place where you nurture what you have, not where you lose it. Whether young or old, set goals aimed at building. If you treat love as your work, success will follow. Love requires readiness from within, not just the influence of peer pressure. Stay grounded in that.

Overcome Social Influences Positively to Move Forward

You are not alone. Someone will always give you ideas on how they succeeded in winning someone's heart. It feels good, but always act with caution.

- How do you deal with daily social influences?

- What impact do they have on your life? Is it positive?

Think about these questions before taking action. You need to learn. Some people have a powerful influence over others.

Once their words are spoken, they can stick to your heart and mind, leading you to follow their advice. Words have great power in love. Not everything they say is bad, but be discerning and use your mind to filter what's best for your new relationship.

Social influences are part of our daily lives. They help us understand our position in life and the stages we're progressing through. When it comes to love, the power of social influence is significant. Most of these influences occur in schools, colleges, workplaces, and peer groups—environments that surround our daily lives. Love benefits from positive social influences. When combined with an active, thoughtful mind, they lead to good decisions. You can't escape social influence during youth, adulthood, or marriage.

Many people listen to what their friends say about love. Some even advise on how to seduce someone and win their heart. However, very few teach you how to maintain that love. If you find someone who does, that's a friend to keep. When you begin a relationship, don't ignore this. Use your mind to determine what positive influences you need at the moment. Sit down and analyze what kind of love you want. While social influences should be heard, don't let them be the key determinants of your life. Whether you're a youth or an adult, take note of this. Train your mind to believe in yourself and what you want in love. Learn to focus.

Write Your Own New Beginning Love Story

Every relationship has its goals. Every new marriage has its principles, set by two committed partners who aim to make their story inspirational not only to themselves but also to those around them. After identifying your new rules to win someone's heart, it's time to start writing your own beautiful love story.

Is your love a feeling or a commitment? What percentage of each category applies to you? Are you able to channel your love more into commitment than just feelings?

Love requires a balance between these two. If one overpowers the other in different situations, trouble will follow. Despite your feelings, nurturing your commitment will help your relationship flourish. You must adhere to this rule. Protect your new partner and channel your feelings into commitment so that he or she can understand your actions.

Communicate with each other as often as possible. This strengthens the desire to be together in all aspects. How you learn in the beginning is how you will maintain the relationship, especially as it progresses toward marriage. Ensure your relationship has a strong foundation before deepening your love. Make sure your partner understands you better than anyone else from the start. She is your guide to your new life of love. Use her as a manual—read and understand her before continuing to build your life together.

A new and better beginning brings courage, joy, hope, perseverance, and a sense of togetherness. Choose her. Choose him. Love her. Protect her. Inspire her. Comfort her. Nurture her. Teach each other until you fully understand how each one thinks and lives.

Take Home Love Message

Believe in yourself. Choose a partner for life. Teach each other as you begin your fresh love journey. Start writing your own love story.

"For He will command his angels concerning you to guard you in all your ways" **Psalm 91:11.**

12

Desire for Togetherness

Love is a journey not to be taken lightly. It's a time when you welcome a new person into your life to complete the other part of yourself. Through that, you will always be together. Togetherness means a lot in love. It doesn't only benefit you but also the next generation.

"Behold, how good and how pleasant it is, for brethren to dwell together in unity." **Psalm 133:1.**

This is a very important aspect that all new couples cherish. Everyone loves to be with his or her spouse, especially in a new relationship. This is a time when emotions run high, and you always want to stay close to your partner. You feel like you want to merge with them, to be with them every moment. Life feels as sweet as nothing else, expressed only through feelings.

Togetherness is an essential element in nurturing your love. Understand its meaning before confidently proclaiming it. Togetherness isn't just about emotions; it's also expressed through your actions. Remember, this is still the beginning of your love journey. The desire for togetherness is a unique characteristic in any new relationship. You will find new couples always together, walking hand in hand, eating out with romantic smiles on their faces, buying each other cards and flowers, and sharing as many romantic moments as possible. That is togetherness.

Every relationship is unique. This phase is special for each couple. It's a time when you get to know each other deeply. It's a time when both partners invest their time to push the love journey forward. Emotions are so high that you don't want anything to separate you. You think about each other all the time.

His or her calls, messages, or pictures become precious gifts to cherish. Any time you hear his or her voice, your heart feels at ease. You even wonder, where was this person all this time? Happiness becomes a daily routine. A smile becomes the language of welcome when you see each other.

Love is a precious gift. You chose that person for a reason. That reason strengthens you and keeps you close. Be ready to understand its meaning before emotions take control of your mind and body. Reflect on these questions to restore and build a strong desire for love:

• How do you see your love journey at the moment? Score yourself, if possible—whether good, bad, or life-threatening—and compare your results with your partner's.

• Is there a positive meaning of togetherness? If yes, assess yourself and score it in percentages to see how well you fit. Be honest with yourself in this task. If no, why not? What's changing your positive meaning of togetherness?

• Are there any changes from the day you began your love journey? What has changed? Are you happy with the results?

• What always unites you the most?

• Invite your partner to ask and answer these questions, and give him or her time to think if needed. Compare your results with your partner.

Do this exercise and score your results. Repeat this exercise periodically to see if the scores improve. Be ready to make corrections early because the journey continues.

Time to Build Your Fresh Love

We all learn every day, and this applies to any kind of new or old relationship. Your togetherness opens another chapter of getting to know each other. It's time to continue building the love you established. It's time to continue building your new house of love.

Transform that gift into a home of love. This journey needs constant strengthening. Focus on that.

Love is like a new house. Each time, you feel the urge to add new furniture. Today, you may bring in a new bed, a couch, a beautiful clothes shelf, a shoe rack, and more. What your mind always thinks of is investing new ideas into your dream house. The same applies to your fresh love. Think to win. Think to cultivate. Think to protect and provide.

If this is how you think, then you should invest more in your spouse. By doing that, your love will always:

- *Protect.*

- *Overcome loneliness.*

- *Encourage.*

- *Tolerate.*

- *Provide peace and harmony.*

- *Focus on the best in each other.*

- *Provide support and comfort.*

- *Motivate and inspire.*

- *Be a home.*

These are your tools to guide your journey. They might have shortcomings, but they are minor at this stage, thanks to your strong desire to know each other. Understand this as it applies to the person you love. It's time to keep building that family of love. Be strong and courageous. No one has ever been superior in love because everyone has a unique way of understanding it.

Do you want to last in love? Focus on your spouse. A new house needs new tools, new ways of maintaining peace and harmony, new ways of sustaining that smile, new ways of learning, correcting, recollecting, and persevering. This is how you build your fresh start for forever endurance. Cherish the good, and leave behind what is of little or no value. Teach each other as you progress. Do not allow loneliness to enter that new home. Have courage because this is your love's rewarding work. Feed your love with a daily desire for togetherness.

Grow Together, Stay Forever

"Yes, I do." Sweet and sensational words from two committed hearts, ready to be tied together forever. A mind focused on one person—your mind when you find the person who means a lot in your life. Say *"I do!"* with an open heart. Be ready to welcome him or her into your heart and mind. Grow together. Take care of each other.

Love is a beautiful story, one that brings desire and intimacy to another person. It gives you new life. It gives you responsibilities. All these must be communicated between you and your spouse. That's why you should always think of growing together with the person who looks perfect in your eyes. Cultivate your relationship. Nourish that love. Find the best nutrients to daily feed your desire for togetherness. By doing that, you will continue growing together.

Look back. Learn. Correct. Hold hands as you pursue forever happiness. Build your commitment.

She loves me, and I love her a lot. We are both busy with work, but we never miss quality time for each other. We may get tired from work, but our love is our number one priority. We always find precious time for ourselves. Sometimes, distance becomes our main barrier, but we find the best ways to communicate. Our love is our number one choice. She is the person I chose, so I must invest in her. I must learn to understand her moods. Despite being complex, she is still my chosen one.

A year ago, after she finished her part-time job at a company, she got a new paying job far from where we used to live. It was difficult to work and stay together for a time. Long distance entered our love life. We decided to live apart for a while. It was very sad, very disappointing to see my wife close the door and say, "I'll see you in six months." I felt like this was a breakup. It was tough in the beginning—coming home from work without her presence. The house seemed silent, as if it didn't know me. No mood for food. Her presence was gone.

It was then that I learned physical distance isn't a total barrier in a relationship. The real distance is in your mindset. I learned new ways to maintain our love despite the physical distance. I made a timetable for how I would communicate with her. That gave me hope. I read many books for inspiration and motivation on how to live in that situation. This strengthened my desire for love. It was then that I realized we need to grow old together. We need to keep staying together, no matter what life throws at us. That's how we overcame physical distance during one of our tough times.

Yes, love needs only one rule to last in that journey: grow together, stay forever. This will always bring the desire to love one another. Don't break that immature chain of love. You're never too old to understand this. When life gives you another chapter to read, be ready to focus with hope. Be ready to read that chapter together. Unite in Jesus' mighty name, and you will find yourself always loving as you continue to grow old.

You Are My Special Valentine

"I won't forget this day. It was the day you gave me a watch and a sweet, lovely card with flowers on top. You moved my heart that day." Beautiful and sweet words on a special day for a special person. How does it feel to hear such words? Is this a dream for you? Good words last forever. A good person cares a lot. He loves what he protects. He knows who his special valentine is in his life. Are you that kind of partner to your spouse?

Your love should have this special day—a day that has positive meaning for you. A day such that when each one remembers, love is restored despite the misunderstandings you might be going through. And that should be your valentine's day. That is the day when your partner is at their peak—a day full of memories and restoration. Be his or her special person on this special day. Dream it, and live it right now. It is time to build your desire for togetherness. Create a strong bond.

"My love, I know you love me a lot. Today is a special day for us. We are celebrating our third anniversary. Thank you for always loving me." Love has surprises and heart-touching words. Once these words are spoken, faith and the desire for togetherness increase. It gives you hope and courage, knowing there's someone who understands your love. Yes, that's your spouse—a perfect match for you, a person willing to share his or her life with you until death separates you.

When building your desire in love, don't forget your commitment. Don't live outside your promises. Your words can heal your partner. Use kind words. Your tone and facial expression will tell the rest. Hold on to that person. Be their special valentine on a special day. Be proud of your spouse. Be proud of yourself. Love is made of a committed desire for togetherness that is created to last forever. If you don't have a gift for your valentine's day, then be their gift. They will understand what that means. Change, and continue living in peace.

Take Home Love Message

Do not underestimate your love. Strengthen your desire and continue moving together.

"Have I not commanded you? Be strong and courageous. Do not be afraid; do not be discouraged, for the Lord your God will be with you wherever you go" **Joshua 1:9.**

Marriage of Your Dreams

Your marriage is your number one job. It is a dream for everyone prepared to take on family responsibilities. Your relationship should not remain just a relationship; it should be elevated to a marriage that is recognized by the whole world. Don't live with that person for a long time without fulfilling the God-given covenant. This is a dream you should always think about. Be ready to live while learning the best about marriage and love.

Dear husband and wife, you both depend on each other. You are like salt in food; when one is missing, the flavor is lost. Do not ignore each other's presence in your beautiful relationship. Depend on each other every day. A good dish is appreciated not only for its appearance but also for its taste. Always be the salt that makes the love taste sweet. Understand the importance of each other in every step of your love journey. Prepare yourself as you continue discovering your spouse toward a successful and happy marriage.

The Covenant Everyone Wants to Make

It was Saturday morning when everyone woke up early, ready for the church mass, to witness these two lovers making their lifelong covenant at the altar. The priest asked her, *"Do you take this man as your husband, to love and obey?"* From a distance, everyone heard a sweet and heartfelt *"yes"* filled with tears. This is the covenant everyone wants to make when deciding to live with the person they love the most. It is the fulfillment of your relationship and the transformation into a married life.

Marriage is a covenant. It is a blessing. If you do not take it seriously, it will become a burden and a curse. It is not for everyone who is an adult; it is reserved for those who are spiritually mature. Do not turn this life gift into nothing. Marry that person and live your commitment. Do not cheat, or make him or her sad. Do not enter this covenant because of money, peer pressure, or age. Pray while learning how to live in marriage. When the right time comes, you will enjoy that gifted life.

The Happy Hours in a Newborn Marriage

A new marriage is like a new hospital. Everyone wants to see how it operates and some even want to take pictures to keep as memories. This hospital is your marriage. Let it be filled with hospitality. Always feel free to invest new positive ideas into running this lifelong partnership. A new marriage is often filled with emotional love. Everyone wants to stay close to each other. During this time, you create your happy hours of commitment and togetherness. Cherish these happy hours because, if you are not careful, they won't last long. Be the one to create and cultivate the marriage of your dreams.

If your wife is cooking, go behind her and hug her, making more love in the kitchen. Be careful of hot flames as they may disrupt everything. If he is off work, welcome him with a beautiful smile and a soft voice to soothe his heart after a long day. A smile is priceless and beneficial to most marriages. Plan a day to relax together on the couch while watching funny and inspirational movies. Create memorable moments.

Marriage gets stronger through the creativity that lives between you. Help each other often in both tough and happy situations. One day, you will remember those happy hours from when you were young in love. Be committed and understand your partner positively. By doing this, you will always be inspired by the spouse you chose to live with.

Know What You Want from Your Spouse

Learning will always keep you safe in your relationship. When two mindsets meet, differences appear as boundaries that grow daily. If you do not address these differences, a gap will continue to grow. Be cautious when resolving differences. It is time to know what you want from your spouse.

- Have you ever quarreled with your beautiful wife or husband?

- What caused the differences?

- Did you manage to resolve them and move on with renewed hope?

- What did you learn?

Ask yourself: Do you know what you want from your spouse at the moment? If you want a lasting relationship, learn to identify what you need. Don't force things; invest in understanding and transforming your mindset.

Knowing what you want from your partner will always keep you safe. Learn the language of love you create each day, whether verbal or non-verbal. Do not say he is too arrogant to listen to your views or always complain about the lack of time. A good partner learns to understand what she wants from her husband.

Remember how you used to talk before marriage. You had so many ways to keep him close. Why has that spirit diminished? What is the gap between you and your spouse? Do you enjoy living in that situation? If you are struggling, you have lost love and the ability to understand what you want from your partner. Rectify this as soon as possible. He or she is important to you. Cherish them by reviewing your needs. Do not let your love decrease.

There are many beautiful people who may catch his attention if you do not invest in him.

List 5-10 things that your spouse might understand as your needs. Do this regularly to track your progress. Aim high and you will find success and confidence. If you succeed, teach your spouse the same.

As a man, love your wife. There is no other rule than loving her. By loving her, you update yourself every day. As a woman, love, learn, and inspire your husband in all he does. This is how you continue holding hands through ups and downs. Quarrels will happen, but let them be steps towards new positive hopes in marriage.

Improve Your Desire Through Sex

In a couple's life, sex is a crucial tool. It brings couples together and, when approached with a positive mindset, elevates your relationship to a higher level of maturity. It is always joyful to have sex with the person you love the most. This becomes even sweeter when fulfilled by your heartfelt partner. That's the true meaning of marital fulfillment.

The world today has turned this gift into business, pleasure, and even a means of revenge. This transformation harms marriages, making them feel like responsibilities rather than self-committed love. Remember, sex should enhance your marriage, not detract from it. If the mood is low, discuss the situation openly. This is your relationship, and it is your number one job.

Sex should never be interpreted negatively. It is the salt that enhances the taste of your marriage. You chose each other for great reasons. Do not cheat on your spouse. Avoid infidelity, as it can bring curses and destroy your marriage. Cherish each other and make good environments to enjoy love through sex. Be creative and learn how to improve your marriage. As a woman, do not be shy, angry, or sad if your partner does not meet your expectations. Understand his preferences. Sex should be a strong connection between you and your partner.

Is Marriage a Final Solution?

Everyone seeks a soulmate to share their love journey. When you think about it, marriage seems like a solution. Is it the final solution for your relationship? Do you enjoy love as you did before, or has something changed after marriage?

The process of marriage has its own excitement. You might think that marriage will solve all your problems. You may believe that this person will love you more once you are married. While this might be true, don't expect marriage to fix everything if you haven't prepared for a fresh start in your relationship. Marriage is a lifelong journey, and if not properly cared for, it may become a fleeting enjoyment. If you wait to love until you are married, you are fooling yourself. Marriage has its happy moments, often most vibrant in the early days.

Dear couple, choose and live with your love partner faithfully, not just in marriage but also before and during courtship. Marriage is not a final solution to your love; it is a continuation of your relationship. You have made a spiritual commitment, but if there's no love, it is not a healthy marriage. Don't use marriage as a bait for attention, wealth, fame, or revenge. Understand the true meaning of marriage before committing to it.

Many have fallen into the trap of misinterpreting this life gift, leading to swift separations and loss of hope. Do not add yourself to that painful list. Learn and correct your ways. Understand why you want to get married and how you will live before and after marriage. Don't rush. Prepare for marriage and enjoy it while cherishing your current relationship. When you succeed, repeat the process.

Take Home Love Message

Live your covenant. Love and protect your beautiful marriage.

"Therefore; what God has joined together, let no one separate" **Mark 10:9.**

Invest in Your Husband

"If I were to change the world, I would start by changing how I love my husband." — **These are the inspirational words of an elderly woman celebrating 20 years of marriage.**

It is every woman's dream to find a man who embodies her ideal qualities: caring, loving, attractive, and a protector of the family. A man who is ready to take full responsibility as a father and husband. This should always be your dream. Make it a reality by investing in your husband. Don't wait—the journey of love awaits your dedicated effort.

Marriage requires daily commitment, which is fulfilled by loving your husband. The man you chose was once very handsome and charming. When you first saw him, you worried that your friends might steal him from you. You would call or text him to check if he had eaten or slept well and to ensure he was taking care of himself. That was your investment. Time has flown by, but you are still together. Is your commitment still the same? Do you still invest in his love? What has changed, that you no longer see his smile?

Love is a choice. The man you love reflects your patience and is a symbol of your relationship. It's time to learn how to invest in him. Be a game changer and approach your love with a positive mindset. Don't be a woman who doesn't think. Be a woman of transformation, one who wants to see her husband excel. Difficulties and misunderstandings won't disappear, but use them as stepping stones toward successful love transformation.

Understand His Love, Weaknesses, and Strengths

Being in a relationship means taking responsibility for growing together. Live by analyzing your man's weaknesses and strengths. Don't aim to destroy; remember, this is your own house of love. He is the man you said yes to when he approached you. Recall how you cultivated your love in the past and how you lived side by side. His problems were yours, and that was when you understood him best. How did that feel? What has changed?

Your husband needs love and respect. He needs your ears and your quality, committed time. Be the best, and let him be the best husband ever. Every man is worth something when taken care of. Treat him like a true king—not just a king by title, but also a king of love and daily respect. Don't underestimate your efforts because the best begins with a single step toward positive transformation. Learn his strengths continually. Understand what he likes most, how he takes care of you, and how he loves his family and children. Be a student while loving your husband. By doing so, you increase the chances of lasting happiness on your journey of love.

Six years ago, I had many troubles with my husband. Our house was filled with quarrels. Each day began with silence between us. It was the hardest time of my life. Our differences were too great, and neither of us was willing to resolve the misunderstandings. Our love was filled with anger, silence, jealousy, and revenge. Despite living together, we ate separately, each person having his or her own time. I felt like breaking up and living alone.

Our family was in total darkness. It was especially difficult for our growing children, particularly John, who was 4 years old. He needed love from his parents, but we had no time for each other or the family. We lived like people who had separated years ago. I even remember a day when we only spoke two words: "Goodnight, dear." Then we slept separately. My husband set his own alarm, and so did I.

One day, I decided to talk to him about our silence, but he avoided the conversation and continued with his work. He didn't want to listen at all. Our children didn't know which side to choose. After a long period of silence, I decided to find a solution to our problem. I read books, visited websites, and listened to online psychologists, though with little hope.

Eventually, I found a great piece of advice about investing in your husband and how to transform and cherish his love despite differences.

After reading those inspirational words, I learned how to turn our silent love back into the passionate love we once shared. I understood his strengths, his weaknesses, and how to turn them into positives. It wasn't a simple or quick process, but a slow and committed journey toward restoration. Men need love. Men need respect. Men need attention. Men need leadership. You need to live side by side. Some days may be tough for him, but those won't last long if you decide to be the change. Learn his good side and his bad side. By doing this over time, we managed to bring back the smile we used to share.

Is your love facing daily challenges that make you feel distant from your husband? Is your life as difficult as this woman's? Every marriage has its ups and downs. Some manage to resolve issues, while others struggle daily. Don't let yourself fall into the latter category. As a woman, you need to understand your husband. List his weaknesses and strengths. Do this exercise daily and monthly. Focus on turning his bad traits into good ones. He is your chosen husband. Don't let him go without a fight. Start now, because tomorrow is a dream that may not come true if you don't prepare for it today.

Being a Smart Wife

Are you proud of the man you love? If you were to marry again, would you choose the same person you're in love with now? Or would you see it as a chance to avoid the mistake of choosing him? Think wisely. He is the one you chose. He is the one who loves you. He is the same man who moved you away from your parents. Be a smart wife. Don't complain that your marriage has lost its spark. Learn how to restore the journey you've lost.

A smart wife knows how to invest in her husband. Why don't you be that kind of woman? There's a saying, *"Behind every successful man, there is a woman."* This is how you should think. This is how you invest in him. Be smart. This is how you'll maintain his smile and his love.

In this journey, you need to restore your faith in him. You need to make him understand that you are the smartest one on earth. You need to let him know that you are beautiful and caring. Give him a reason why he chose you over other women. Don't just be a girl—be a woman, be a wife. Don't live lightly.

If he is working on his job, business, or projects, be his number one supporter. Don't let him down. Be active and cooperate with his aspirations. If he stays quiet for a long time, find a sweet way to bring back his smile. Don't ignore his low mood—focus on that too.

If he wants to learn new things about the family, be his teacher and guide him. Teach him how to care for the children, cook, and spend quality time with the family. Teach him how to love you in tough times. If he likes spending time with his friends, don't argue or quarrel. Understand his life. Show him how love should be lived between you. Don't devalue his status. Guide him in a better way. Show him the path you want to take together.

If he treats you poorly, stay calm. Meditate. Relax. This difficult time will pass, and hope will return. Focus on building your love despite the challenges. Remind him who he is to you.

Help your husband financially when necessary. Don't separate—be a winning team. Grow together in love, and also economically. Be proud of his success in business. Motivate him whenever he is at home.

Men have dark days at work. Sometimes they skip meals to provide for their families. They even forget to take care of themselves to ensure the family is well. Don't despair if you go through such a lifestyle. Love is a journey, and these are just part of it. Be a smart wife.

Your Faith is Your Commitment

Do you love your marriage? Then increase your faith in the person you love. Marriage is a covenant that should not be broken. Your husband is the only person who fulfills that role. He is your life companion. Start by always investing in him. Increase your faith by loving and protecting him. Don't see yourself as weak. Be strong, and you'll find hope as you continue cherishing that man. He is your king, not your servant.

Be committed to the precious time he invests in you. When he brings something to the family, be there to accept and support him. Don't take his money for granted—you're building one house together. He is there to protect you. He is your husband and a father of your children. Be one unit, and your love will grow day by day. Don't let him be lonely. Let him be the reason for your love. Whatever you do, do it with love and the mindset of growing together. This is your committed journey. Never look back. Keep investing in the positivity of your husband.

Promise and Live Your Words

Most men work hard to provide for their families. This is the number one rule for a responsible man. By doing so, distance may sometimes come between you and your husband. There will be times when he has to leave home for work, and he will be lonely and miss you. His presence may diminish if you don't focus on him. You may forget the promises you made when you began your love journey. During such times, pray and live by your words. Surrender to God for His guidance, protection, and help.

Your words should encourage, motivate, and remind him of the path you've taken together. Remind him of the life of love you've chosen. Tell him that despite the distance, you will overcome the challenge. Your love will continue to shine, and your promises will live on day by day. Being a wife doesn't just mean taking care of children. It means being the second pillar of the family after your husband. Support him in tough and happy times. Remind him that tomorrow will be another day of everlasting happiness. Don't wait— prepare for it right now.

Don't cheat on your husband. Don't mock him when he's gone. Don't lie to your children that you're the hero in everything. Don't take all the credit. This isn't a competition of who wins or fails. Remember, you are one family. Learn and correct your thinking.

Understand his roles and weaknesses. Marriage is life. Be alive and keep guiding your husband toward loyalty. Increase your intimacy so that he will miss you and the family when he is away for work. Embrace his actions.

Take Home Love Message

Love your husband. Encourage and protect what he invests in your family.

"For the husband is the head of the wife, as Christ also is the head of the church, He Himself being the savior of the body" **Ephesians 5:23.**

Invest in Your Wife

Loving your wife deeply? Yes, always invest in her. As each day begins, remember to invest in her love—a love that's open and understandable. Focus on this, and you will find joy in your marriage.

Love is a gift, a gift meant to be shared—not with ego or jealousy, but with intimacy and humility. All these qualities can be found in the one person who captures your heart. And that person should always be your wife. Whether today or tomorrow, she is the one deserving of your love. Now is the time to boost that love by investing in her. This is a daily task. Whatever you do, do it with love. Strive to win her heart always.

Why Do You Need to Invest in Your Wife?

Life is unpredictable. If you remember where you came from and the journey you've been on, your wife will become the number one priority in your life. It was a long time ago—perhaps months or years—when she was just a pretty girl who made your heart race whenever you saw her.

Her presence became your cure, despite having no disease to suffer from. It's funny when you remember those days. You even recall the many promises you made to elevate her on this wonderful earth. Yes, that was you—a person filled with passionate love. But is your love still the same? Do you still invest in her? Why?

On this journey, you need to learn and refine your love. Embrace the positivity of investing in your spouse. She may have changed— maybe she's now a bit heavier, skinnier, older, crazier, or more eccentric—but she is still yours. Time changes, and so does she. She is the same girl who touched and captured your heart, the same person you married years ago.

Now, it's history. The beauty you once sought may have faded, but does she seem like a different person to you? Is that a reason not to love her as you used to? No—do not look with a negative mind. It's time to cherish and nurture your love. Look within yourself and find a way to win her heart again. That's how you will invest in your caring love. Love is togetherness.

In my book titled **Another Side of Love**, I have clearly explained how you can nurture and rekindle your love in just **22 days,** so you can always move forward together with your partner. Each day offers lessons to help you close your day with a positive lesson from your spouse.

Love is a journey—a journey that takes commitment, patience, and forgiveness. This journey may seem simple to hear about but is complex to live through. Be the one to know your wife's needs. Be the one to understand her emotions, pain, loneliness, sadness, and happiness. Once you've mastered these, you will always be her number one comfort zone. Learn the importance of investing in someone who means so much in your life. Your wife is your other side of love.

Family is the greatest gift in life. The girl who is now your wife is a very important person to accompany you on this love journey. Love her. Protect her. Pray for her. Support her in whatever she does. By doing this, you will always invest in her love. Reflect on these questions:

- Is your wife still the most important person in your life? Does this feeling still live within you with a high degree of positivity?

- Are you proud of your beautiful wife? Are you happy when she does something that deserves appreciation and thanksgiving? Or does that feel like a distant dream?

- Why do you need to invest in your wife? What is this investment that you want to make?

• Is your love facing challenges, misunderstandings, or a sense of regret? Is your wife the cause of all these?

• What memories or events have had a great impact and taught valuable lessons in your life, showing you how your wife has transformed you?

One day, ask her these questions and let her explain how you've invested in her up to this moment. Compare her answers with yours. If possible, write them down and keep them as a memory. Aim for the best. Learn and continue transforming yourself into a caring and responsible husband.

When love feels like a routine, your journey enters a phase of testing. You may feel like she's changed, that she doesn't follow your desires or understand your love language. But this is because life presents you with a new chapter—to think about how to cherish the woman you love. Understand that love transitions from youth to old age. Following this path of love means facing ups and downs, which is why you need to find ways to continually win her heart.

The Benefits of Investing in Your Wife

• You grow into positivity towards love and romance. You understand that without her, you are incomplete, and this realization strengthens the journey you began together.

• You transform her understanding of love into something daily and enduring. You give her room to appreciate and respect your care. Once you understand her, she learns how to love you in return. You teach her that two are better than one.

• You turn conflicts into opportunities. You recognize that everything that happens in your love is a lesson to be learned. This perspective helps you push through tough times.

• By investing in her, you turn love into a partnership. This should be your routine, not just a dream. Work as partners in everything you do—whether it's business, prayers, housework, or taking care of the children. Let her be your number one supporter.

• You teach your children that family is love. They see this love in their mother, whom they call "Mom." This maintains peace and harmony within the family and shows your children that you are a great icon of love and support.

• You and your wife can sit down and reflect on your journey together. Analyze where you've been and where you want to go. Don't wait. Plan your love journey as you grow older. Correct your mistakes and restore the hope she once placed in you. Be the change.

Remember, *a wife is life, but if not cared for enough, she can become a knife and cut off your life.* Escape this fate. Let her sharpen your life, and you will always prosper in whatever you do as a family.

Continue strengthening your journey—there are still many more years to come.

Nurturing Your Wife

Everyone has a list of things that bring them joy, especially in times of stress, bad moods, or loneliness. This might come from music, movies, sports, or exploring different places in this beautiful world. These activities bring peace and restore us to our better selves.

Being in a relationship means growing together through tough and sweet situations. This journey comes with a positive approach to nurturing your wife by investing in her love. One day, take a piece of paper or a notebook and write down your list of things that make you happy. Keep it as a record. Does that list include your wife as part of your happiness and peace? If not, now is the time to learn how to nurture your wife and channel her into becoming one of the best people in your life—the best person in your world of love.

Learn how to nurture your wife. Create a special list of love for yourself. Write down the things you're going to invest in her. Start with two or more and continue discovering her importance in your life. Make that list special, with a positive focus. This should be a daily, weekly, and monthly task. Don't ignore this life-changing practice.

Does your wife love surprises? If yes, then do more with love and respect.

Does your wife like you to be at home and help with housework? Then do it with commitment.

Does she like watching television or movies with you? Don't ignore that. Learn to appreciate it.

Does she like to manage the family's finances? Be her assistant and an active listener.

Does she like to pray together with you and the children? Don't find excuses to avoid the word of God. Be there. Pray together with hope.

Does she like to work on new projects or investments that you don't even have a clue about? Be her number one supporter. Teach and correct with positivity. This brings motivation and confidence.

Do all these questions seem like a dream or a miracle to you? If yes, then repeat them and do the right thing to nurture your wife. If no, then continue strengthening your bond. Learn her.

By following these principles, you will always find the best ways to cherish your wife. You will grow together with a positive mindset each day. You will become the best husband ever. Your wife is a reflection of your commitment.

Always find ways to invest in her. Compare your current list with the previous one and see the improvements you've made. That's how you continue loving each other each day.

Be a proud husband. Be an inspiration. That's your wife. You chose her for a lifetime reason. Don't change your mind. Focus on the best.

The Inspirational Husband

Dear husband, marriage is a continuation of your relationship. You need to continue protecting that woman. Trust yourself as you fulfill your roles. Life might not be the same as it used to be. Some days, your woman might get sick. Learn the household chores like cooking, feeding the children, washing clothes, staying at home with the family, and other activities. This should be your new dream. Don't just provide basic needs. A husband is a man who is fully responsible for his family—from providing to spending quality time with his family.

If you want to be a successful husband, be inspirational. Be positive. Be courageous. Be creative. Another way to become inspirational is to be responsible for your family, and don't think of running away in difficult moments. As you were the one to marry her, you must continue protecting her. Don't let negativity rule your mind. There is light at the end of the tunnel. Let positivity lead you to new changes in your life.

Always look at your family and marriage as a daily dream that needs you to be focused, committed, responsible, and creative in order to live it. Keep your relationship strong. Always dream about what makes you proud of your family. How do you want your family to look in the coming years? What makes you proud to be a husband? Do you think you can do better than yesterday?

Don't be confused. Take action. Start dreaming today. Write down how you want to invest in your wife. Don't ignore your daily responsibilities—fulfill them with pride. Dream of a new family transformation that will be filled with love, respect, and thanksgiving. That's what you need to succeed in your love journey.

Cherish the Moment

Your marriage is filled with memories—moments that tied you together from courtship to your current married life. These moments, when remembered, bring daily happiness, solving the hunger of loneliness. Despite being married, your love is still a work in progress. Don't forget the good memories that led to your current life. Love moves forward with positive moments. Don't just count them; let them be strong pillars of your life.

Life happens now. Make her your queen. Never forget the day you made your commitment—the day that set you on this love journey. Cherish every moment; that's the real life you need to live each second. Ups and downs will accompany you on this path. Understand this. Be proud of your wife—she's the same person you dated long ago.

Don't scold her. Don't ignore her. Don't make her sad. Silence won't solve anything; it provides only temporary relief but creates a lifelong problem. Be the change and rekindle that passionate love.

Have you ever avoided home to escape her presence? Remember, love is home. Be a home to your wife. Let her miss you when you're away. Create peaceful environments. Teach her to understand your caring love. Sit close as you once did.

Remind each other of the best moments that transformed your lives. Plan for the future, beginning now. Cherish every moment. That's how you invest in your beautiful wife. Will you do that?

Take Home Love Message

Teach your wife how to be a home of love for the family. Love her with all your heart.

"Let your fountain be blessed, and rejoice in the wife of your youth" **Proverbs 5:18.**

The praying marriage

"Two are better than one, because they have a good reward for their toil. For if they fall, on one will lift up his fellow. But woe to him who is alone when he falls and has not another to lift him up!" **Ecclesiastes 4:9-10 — That's how you should always move in your marriage.**

When you unite, God makes you firm in everything you do. Do it with love. Do it with compassion. Do it with a sense of total forgiveness. Be courageous, and you will always transform your relationship into a daily church of love.

Your spouse is your disciple. Together, you make a home of prayers. If you want to succeed in what you are doing, then pray together.

Be a praying marriage. Pull each other through many temptations. Do not leave one behind. Invest in that. If you pray, everything becomes clear. It shows you a mistake and a solution to rectify it. God blesses people who have a positive mindset. Do not lose this favor. Loving your wife is another way of praying.

It is time to pray; pray together

One day, wake up early in the morning. Prepare everything as you can. Hold your wife's hand as you leave the house. Do not forget your Bible. Walk courageously towards the church. Find a sweet and perfect place to sit together. Let the fresh air come in and comfort both of you. Promise yourself that today, you are going to listen to the Word of God together until the end of the mass. Listen as the priest continues preaching the Word of God. Note down some key verses if possible. When the mass is finished, leave the same way you came from home.

Marriage needs daily prayers. These are the nutrients that continue nurturing your committed journey. As a couple, pray together. There is no other rule on that.

- How do you feel after staying close to your wife during the mass?

- Does that seem like a dream now? What has changed then?

- How do you pray in your marriage?

- Is God living among you, or do you seek Him only when troubles begin to be your companion?

When it is time, pray together. That is how you move with positivity. That is how you daily renew your covenant. Prayers have strong power to protect and guide any marriage that seeks God's grace. Find your best time and do not forget to teach your partner how to pray as you do. Let your successes be filled with prayers before and after. If you understand that, then:

- Pray before and after meals.

- Pray for your family.

- Pray for your togetherness as you continue getting older.

- Pray for your projects, work, businesses, talents, and any investment you are working on.

- Pray before and after traveling.

- Pray that success, poverty, wealth, and any tough time may never be a source of downfall in your marriage.

- Pray that you may always stick together in happy and tough situations you might pass through.

- Pray for whatever you are doing.

Love is strengthened by working prayers. When you have troubles or misunderstandings, pray and work towards a better resolution. No relationship is perfect, which is why perfection is completed by working prayers. As a couple, pray with hope. Be one unit. Let your success be filled with the Word of God. Do not live blindly. Start to pray now and protect your marriage.

Living your true love; Be an angel

Dear couple, love is created to last forever. Your commitment, your time, and your mind should always rest on the Word of God. Marry and live with a partner who understands this principle.

Live with that person who has fear and respect for God's ways. That is the person whom you should train every day. Be her angel, and he will be your saint. Together, you will make your marriage a home of prayers. You will make a small church that always praises the Lord. You will always enjoy the marriage you prayed for.

Living your true love is something that you should always be proud of. Pray with total faith. Pray for your husband. Pray for your kids. Go inside your room, close all the doors, and pray with faith.

Pray until you feel the inner energy coming out of you. Involve your husband in such a ceremonial prayer. Teach him if he doesn't understand. Rectify if possible. When you move, move together. Not only in works, but also in prayers. That's how you become a praying marriage.

Love your spouse, love yourself!

Marriage is a tough journey if not taken care of. It becomes a huge barrier that separates both of you daily. Every day, you will find new negative mindsets to put on your partner. You will feel like you got him or her for free. You will start to lose his or her value each day.

Everyday life gives you something bad about your spouse. If you continue living that way, then you proceed towards dishonesty, unfaithfulness, and a path towards total breakup. Why live that kind of life? Was that your purpose before you got married?

In order to succeed and transform your marriage, you need to invest in prayers. You need to love yourself. That is how you will find time to pray while loving that handsome husband. That is how you stay faithful to your wife. All these need to be communicated. Love yourself. Love what you always pray for. A good marriage needs daily nourishment.

If you want to last long, start by loving yourself daily. That is how you will love your husband. That is how you will always stay faithful. Do not cheat on her. You began that journey with God, so live and finish it together in God's grace.

Confess your sins. Be faithful

If you are ready to love, then be ready to confess your sins. There are times when you will quarrel until you can't listen to each other. Your life will be full of stress, disappointment, and more sins. This is the right time to confess your sins. Call her with a soft voice. Tell her what you did. Tell her what went wrong until you didn't want to hear her voice again. Be calm and unleash your anger.

Love needs commitment. Being faithful is a positive way of confessing your sins. It is a restorative way of maintaining your love. It is a sign of reconciliation. A sign of repentance. Learn that act of love.

Confession is the best prayer that should live in your sweet marriage. Do this act each and every time. Let it be your habit. By doing that, you increase your faith in that husband you chose to live with. That is how you should pray. That is how you strengthen your bond.

If you want peace and happiness to rule your family, then confess your deeds. Let each other understand that perfection has no place in your heart. You need each other to complete the cycle of love. Tell your partner that today is a day of confession. I will listen to you, and you will listen to me. Our aim is to move forward from our mistakes. Our aim is to never repeat similar mistakes that separated us before. Promise yourself that, this time, God will be your guide. Have hope and learn to move into a new house of learning and forgiveness.

"If I were to tell you that love really exists, no one would have believed me. Not only my friends, but also my relatives. They didn't believe when I was young, teaching and preaching about love. When I started this journey of marriage with my beautiful wife, everyone thought I wouldn't last long. Some told me that she is not my only woman.

When I traveled far away for work, others would take her. These words became like a national anthem where I used to live.

Life is very funny, my friend. What made me live that long with my wife was working prayers. This was our motto. We prayed that God may prevent us from breaking our covenant we made in front of people. We made sure our confession became our rule towards forgiveness.

Today, I'm an old man with more wisdom, and most people come to learn through me about love and endurance. My son, continue writing your beautiful story concerning love and marriage. But all in all, never abandon the woman you chose to live with."

Your love is your choice. Live like the words of this old man; make your own love story. Cherish it. Pray for it each and every working day. Correct it when necessary. Move together and grow old forever.

Take home Love message

The marriage that prays together, stays together. Confess your deeds, and peace will be your home.

"Therefore, confess your sins to one another and pray for one another, that you may be healed. The prayer of a righteous person has great power as it is working." **James 5:16.**

Invest in Your Children

Is love alone enough? How do you live with your children? Love teaches and protects what is best for you. This is the kind of love you should always consider.

You've been together in your relationship for a while, and now you have children—blessings from God. When you go home, you see them as signs of your future generation. This journey reminds you of another, more perfect place to invest.

Your love is not enough if you do not invest in your children. Life is unpredictable. You might be living with your children, providing daily necessities, but failing to teach them the meaning of love.

You do not create an environment for them to understand that gift. They live, but do not understand how to love and care. Consider these scenarios:

• You love your wife, but you do not show it in front of your children. At home, you don't stay close to her. You always have time for yourself, and your children see you as a lonely person in the house. What do you think they will ask in their minds?

• Your days are full of conflicts. You shout. You ignore your spouse's presence in front of your children. Your conflicts become so evident that even the children notice.

• You used to eat together in the dining room, but now that is history. Everyone has his or her own time for meals. Even your children know that when the food is ready, everyone will eat separately. Is that the kind of love you want? Is that the kind of love you teach your children?

• No kind words come out of your mouth concerning love. You feel as though life forced you to live with that person. You even shout until your children hear your differences. Does this still trouble you? Is harsh language now your primary means of communication? Why?

• Your differences have grown so significant that you decided to divide the children between yourselves. Each parent decides to care for the child they prefer. The mother takes the son, and the father takes the daughter. Everything from school needs to other necessities is now handled separately. Where does your conflict go then? Why are your children being involved in your conflict?

If you are experiencing any kind of conflict that is unhealthy for you and your children, be ready to find a positive solution as soon as possible. Be prepared to correct, restore, and move forward with positive influences on your children. Every child is a blessing—a blessing to cherish. Your child reflects how you live with your partner. He or she may seem like just a child, but very special. Do not underestimate that love. Being in love with your spouse means transforming your life into a better future generation—a generation of hope, positivity, love, and care. Aim for that, my friend.

These scenarios show that if you do not channel your love well, you cannot escape a heartbroken life—a miserable life despite fulfilling daily needs. Change your perspective and invest in your children. Teach them what love is and how to express it. Remember, they learn from what you do, say, and how you act in front of them.

Live and Teach Your Children

I know you love that man. I know he means everything to you. You chose him over others for many reasons. You used to smile whenever you saw him. He conquered your heart without climbing any walls. You set your goals, and now here you are, with children who resemble you. They symbolize your committed journey of love. So, why are you not investing in the right place? Don't they mean love to you? Why doesn't the life you are living provide any positive lessons for your children? It's time to teach them better.

Before you proceed with learning and transforming your perspective, take note of this. Write down scenarios that do not symbolize love in your family. This may be difficult, but try. Even listing two scenarios might change your life. You do not have to be in a situation where your children witness daily conflicts. After writing those scenarios, ask yourself what your children are learning from you. Is there love? Is it enough? Where do you need to correct?

Taking care of your spouse is not as easy as you think. Relationships are full of daily challenges. If you do not learn to understand them, they will strike your family, separate you from your children, and create a boundary that blocks positivity from your family. You will lose recognition of love from your partner, and even from your children. You will live a life of shame, becoming a father who buys things for his family without love, merely fulfilling his responsibilities. You will be a mother who cooks and does housework as a routine, with no love for her family. Be a game-changer and focus on transforming your children into positive individuals.

Remember what you should not do in front of your children:

• Slapping your wife in front of your children.

• Yelling at your spouse. Be mindful of your tone, words, and facial expressions, as children pick up on these quickly.

• Avoiding family meals together in the dining room, as you used to. It may seem minor, but be cautious!

• Ignoring your spouse's presence in front of your children when they need you.

• Speaking hurtful words to your spouse in front of your children. These words affect them day by day. Be careful!

• What other things should not be done in front of your children? List them here and commit to implementing them.

Love focuses on the best. In this journey, learn and keep investing in your children. Your daily life serves as lessons for them. Be an inspirational father or mother. Teach them how to become better partners and positive parents in the future. Do not always complain; instead, focus on building a better future for your children. Let them understand that love is family and family is love. That should be your motto. By doing this, you increase the chance of loving each other, and your life will motivate them every day. They will learn how to love in the future.

Note your daily differences with your spouse and resolve them in a way that your children do not notice. That is how you teach them to be good and responsible parents. Your life is a mirror to your children. Do not create too many cracks in it. Fix them and move forward. It is not a simple task, but believe that you will win, and continue growing old together confidently.

One day, take your children outside the house. Go to a beautiful place—maybe a beach, hotel, hiking spot, restaurant, daycare center, or cave. Let them play as much as they want. While they play, find a perfect spot and sit down with your spouse. Ask them these simple, life-changing questions:

- How is our love life now?

- Do you think we are good parents?

- Do we teach our children positive lessons about love and family?

- Where did we go wrong, leading our children to learn negatively?

- What is our plan for improvement?

After listening to the answers, write them down in a notebook or on your phone, and let them guide you toward new love. That is how you build a strong relationship and strengthen your commitment. Focus on your children. Teach them well. Love is not enough if you do not invest in your children, and this is how you should invest.

After listening to your spouse, find time to ask your children about love. Ask them what love means to them and what they learn from you. Be keen to listen. Lower your defenses. Open your ears and let them teach you, if necessary. That is how you journey with hope.

Children need love, and that love will also build yours. Never underestimate it. Some people lack love because they were not loved as children. That lifestyle shaped their minds until they became parents themselves. Do not let that affect your children. Love should never be taken lightly.

The best spouses understand what their children should learn from them. They know that love extends beyond themselves and includes their children. By doing this, they continue to unite and love each other every day.

Be happy with the family you have. Know where to invest. But always invest in your children. Teach them how to be the best parents in the future. Teach them how to be successful couples. Together, hold hands with faith. Love your children, and you will find that your relationship prospers day by day. You started that journey of love; strengthen your bond, and God will do the rest.

Before you finish this journey, remember these eleven rules to teach your children:

---

1. Teach your children how to love and respect.

2. Teach your children how to care.

3. Teach your children how to be responsible parents.

4. Teach your children how to think positively in everything.

5. Teach your children how to take care of themselves as they grow up.

6. Teach your children not to judge others' lives.

7. Teach your children how to grow economically and financially.

8. Teach your children how to pray.

9. Teach your children how to forgive and forget.

10. Teach your children the true meaning of family.

11. Teach your children how to understand your love.

Love is not selfish. Love is home. Love is learning. Love is a powerful tool to live with. Let your spouse understand this meaning as you communicate with your children. Do not be alone in this. Find good ways to make your children happy and help them understand how you love each other.

By doing so, you strengthen the bond between you and increase positivity in your family. Always end your day with inspiration from your actions. Move forward together. This is a journey of love. Despite having children, your relationship is ongoing.

Do not forget that! Cherish and cultivate it in the best way. Nurture your children with love and humility.

Take Home Love Message

Strengthen your love by investing in your children. Let them be icons of your caring and committed love.

"Discipline your children, and they will give you peace; they will bring you the delights you desire" **Proverbs 29:17.**

Parenthood Love

Family is love. It is a home for everyone. This requires parents who have a strong bond with each other, parents who understand each other.

This journey comes to teach and remind you that parenthood is a very important period to continue nurturing your relationship. Being a parent means taking on multiple responsibilities. But that doesn't mean you should decrease your love for that beautiful woman.

Your journey is still in process towards everlasting happiness. If you dream of becoming a better parent, do not forget to care for the person you chose to live with.

- Are you a responsible parent to your children?

- Do you give them enough time?

- How does it feel after becoming a parent? Does parenthood have negative effects on your relationship?

- Are your children a source of closeness in your marriage? What has changed?

- What is your workup? Are you ready for a positive change?

Relationships have phases. There are times when you will enjoy your love to the maximum and times when things will go down. During these phases, you always need to have a new working plan to push your relationship to maturity. Despite being a parent, your husband or wife should always be the same person you think of. Parenthood challenges should not separate you; they should make you stronger. You can do it!

Learning and Loving Your Parenthood

Being a parent is a blessing from your active loving relationship—a love that is positive and fruitful, fulfilled by having children who act as icons of your commitment. During this period, you need to learn while continuing to love your spouse. Cherish and invest in positive transformation towards daily success.

Having children and other home responsibilities should always make you a better person each day. They should often make you happy and always remind you of the covenant you made when you said "Yes!"

Dear couple, if you are not careful, the parenthood season may make you enemies. It can separate you day by day. You might find yourself taking care of children and forgetting to give quality care to your relationship. You may feel that your partner doesn't deserve your attention at the moment, and he or she only needs to fulfill his or her role as a husband or wife. Everyone will generate his or her own new rules, and priorities will shift. Does this happen among you? Do you use this season as an escape plan from your beautiful spouse?

Being a parent is not an easy task. Imagine taking care of your children and simultaneously your husband. Cooking awaits you, cleaning the house, washing dishes, taking care of that newborn, and other remaining tasks. When you finish all these activities, the pleasure of staying with your loved husband is reduced. You may feel like staying alone for a while. But your partner needs your time and attention. How do you deal with that?

Also, think of a man waking up early in the morning and going to work from morning to evening. His day is filled with tough and thinking work. Sometimes, he returns home with little or no money for family needs. All these are daily duties to run his family. It is still a challenge.

Caring for your partner is your daily job. He or she is a lifetime supporter, your forever person, whether in good or bad days. This includes the season of parenthood, where each one is trying his or her best to cope with new life rules. This season should teach, unite, and always make you happy. Children or other responsibilities will never leave you; they are part of your life. Solve them with positive efforts. Love your spouse, love your parenthood. Be the change and strengthen your bond.

I remind you to love your parenthood. Love all the stages life takes you through. Love being a happy parent. Live and love all responsibilities that make you a man of God. Be a parent but also a responsible man of love. Love your spouse and yourself. Find more time and plan on how you are going to push that love boat. Together, make your relationship a learning class not only for yourself but also for your growing children.

Be United Through Your Children

Children are the best icons of the family. They link single-parent families to nuclear and even extended families. They symbolize the growth of your relationship and show the maturity of your journey. These are key individuals in every family. If you understand their importance, your relationship will have a key link in both tough and happy times. Let them be a blessing, not a curse.

- Are you connected through your children?

- Do they bring joy and happiness to your marriage?

- Are your children the source of your togetherness?

- Do you love that person because he or she has a child with you? Is that an umbrella you have been using to capture that person?

- What happens if you lose all your children? Will your love for that person fade away?

Love can sometimes be a tough journey. You began that journey as two, and now you have children. The family keeps growing. Be united through your children. Date a woman who is ready to be a wife and handle all responsibilities—not only as a queen in the house but also as a mother of your children. She will provide love to you and your children and be a good link between you and your upcoming generation. That is how you get connected to your children. A man of God knows his blessings and never takes for granted what is important to him. This is a husband who should take care of his children and love you with all his heart. Do not live with a man simply because he bore a child with you. Find a man who fears God, understands his values as a husband and a partner. He will care for your children and ensure you always stay connected despite the ups and downs.

Remember, love is not for everyone who is not prepared for it. Understand your time and move on with faith. Do not be a parent if you will not fulfill your duties. By doing so, you will not love your partner and will lose your love for her. You will not feel the importance of being a responsible parent. Your children will become a barrier separating you and your beautiful wife. Life will make you feel unworthy of being with that person. If that condition continues, your parenthood love will be completely destroyed, ending your committed love journey. Do not end up in that depressive stage. Change for the best.

Your children should symbolize peace and restoration. They should strengthen your marriage. Learn and enjoy your parenthood love. Find new ways to live in peace while caring for your children. Enjoy your love while being a parent. Make your committed time and teach each other what kind of love you want to have.

Make Your Own Parenthood Rules

Every family has its rules. What about yours? This principle should also apply to you. Love needs rules. These rules make you stronger and more committed to what you do. After knowing each other for a long time in your relationship, it's now time to formulate your new principles. Principles that will guide you from the present to the future. Principles that will keep you respected, committed, and always thinking of each other.

Lack of respect is a source of misunderstandings and daily quarrels among couples. Do not take it for granted. Do not take each other lightly. Be one unit and plan what kind of rules you are going to live by. They will help you maintain your love life through various seasons. Focus on that, and your journey will always prosper. If that is what you should think of, remember these key rules of better parenthood love:

- Love yourself and your efforts

- Always love your spouse

- Love your children

- Love your marriage

- Love your parenthood lifestyle

- Create positive endurance skills in your relationship

- Never leave your family in happy or tough times

A love that is fruitful has its visions and missions—a vision that should not only live through itself but also extend to future generations. This should be your marriage: a connected marriage from husband to children. Be positive. Live within your rules. Make your wife proud of you and be proud of yourself. These rules will act as guidance on how to continue loving each other. They will always remind you of your covenant. Your love is your job. Without rules, you will fail, fall, and give up.

Love in a Loud Voice

A voice of love should always be shared among you. It should unite you as you grow older. Marriage is a happy place. Say the words of love frequently, not only to your spouse but also to your children. Let them hear you with an active and smiling face. Let them understand your language of communication. When you are at home, show them love and care. Call your wife with a smiling face.

Being a parent doesn't mean you shouldn't focus on your partner. Your husband needs you just as much as your children do. Everyone wants to have quality time with you. This is the perfect time to speak love in a loud voice—a voice meant to be shared, not to discriminate against the people you love the most. As a parent, learn this skill. If your spouse needs you, find a sweet way to listen. It not only builds and strengthens your relationship but also teaches your children. That is how you should live.

Share your parenthood responsibilities and be committed to your action plan. If it involves schooling, work together toward that. If she needs help with cleaning the house while caring for the newborn, be there to help. If he is out cleaning the backyard, make sweet and flavorful food. Be connected through multitasking at home. Love is a daily learning task. It doesn't favor superiority or inferiority complexes and doesn't require any form of fame among you. Love to learn and learn to love. By doing so, you will always enjoy the love you get from the beautiful partner you chose to commit your life to.

Dealing with the Loss of a Child

Love has ups and downs. Some are very easy to deal with, and others are very painful and difficult to handle. Your marriage is strong, and God has given you children who love and obey what you teach them. However, bad news can hit your marriage—one of your children may die. It might be a sudden death or a prolonged illness until death meets him or her. This is a very heart-wrenching and sad situation to endure. Whether married or not, you need to learn how to overcome such a tough and heartbreaking moment.

The loss of a child can also lead to the downfall of your marriage. This situation can separate you and make you lifetime enemies. Remember, every couple is united through their children. If you are not careful, during these tough times, new conflicts may arise and separate the bond you've made. You may feel like you have nothing left to share. All of your love may seem to have been transferred to that child, leaving nothing to share with your partner. Your mind may be filled with thoughts and disappointments. As you navigate this moment, be calm and let life teach you new positive rules of parenthood love.

Love is the first rule to live by. This rule applies not only during happy times but also during heartbreaking moments. It gives you hope and new inspiration to mend the broken bond through the loss of your child. You do not know what tomorrow will bring, but you can prepare for it. Maintain your love with your partner, whether you have children or not. Love should never be broken by temporary circumstances. Love your wife. Love your children. Love yourself.

Death brings change, which is always very tough. Be wise. Be strong. Hold and hug each other. Be one unit as you remember your vows at the altar. God is teaching you something new. Help your partner as she continues to recover from this emotional blow. Do not make major decisions during this season. Prioritize your marriage. Learn and move forward with hope. Avoid divorce and constant fighting. Understand your spouse and be ready to handle this difficult time. Love is a journey, and this journey reminds you to always love and protect what you have. Be the change, and God will provide new positive ways to love as you live.

Enjoy Your Love Through Family Planning

Love goes hand in hand with proper family planning. This is another key rule you should always consider. If you want to spend love properly with your partner, understand the benefits of family planning.

———————

• What does family planning mean to you?

• How do you feel when you hear these words?

• Do you still enjoy the love you have with your wife?

• What gaps do you want to address? Is family planning one of them?

———————

A relationship is strengthened by quality time. Through that, you can plan and review where you came from and where you want to go. To enjoy the gift of love, you need to understand the proper meaning of family planning. This will heal your marriage and give you more room to enjoy your togetherness despite having children.

Love itself is not enough if you do not consider proper family planning. Is your partner going to the maternity ward each year? Do you treat her like a production machine? No, that is not good. Sit down and plan how to space your children. Give yourselves enough room to think about how to have children. Space them out so you can enjoy parenthood and quality time as a couple.

Family life involves being responsible as both a parent and a partner. To enjoy your love, plan your life now. Plan your parenthood. Don't forget to love your spouse. Have time for your children but also time for your spouse.

Understanding family planning will prevent other preventable lifestyle issues. Consider the following:

• Various methods you can use to prevent unwanted and unplanned pregnancies. Learn modern methods such as injectables, implants, or intrauterine devices (IUCDs) that have longer effects and are less costly. Don't forget daily methods to prevent unplanned pregnancies. Know your partner's cycle calendar, when she is fertile, and when she isn't. Do not be shy; learn this now!

• Know your age and health. As a couple, seek regular medical check-ups. This habit will give you confidence and more knowledge about reproduction and how to take care of each other. You will learn what women need and what you should always consider regarding parenthood and love. Knowing your age will help you decide how many children you want at the moment and understand the risks of having more children in a short time. This is love—a love that understands what is crucial for each other. Cherish it.

• Avoid preventable sexually transmitted infections (STIs). This is another crucial aspect of love. Family planning goes hand in hand with preventing infections. These infections, like HIV, pelvic infections, and syphilis, can destroy your love and make you lose hope and faith in your partner. Be wise and faithful. Protect and nurture your marriage.

Dear couple, your love is a golden gift on this Earth. Do not take it for granted. Learn positively, be faithful to each other, and be committed to your plans. Learn and push that love to old age. Plan and live with hope. That's how you will love each other despite being parents. It's time to create more memories in your life journey.

Take Home Love Message

Live by your committed rules during parenthood. Never leave your house in tough times.

"By wisdom a house is built, and through understanding it is established; through knowledge its rooms are filled with rare and beautiful treasures." **Proverbs 24:3-4.**

Learning from Your Memories

Love brings surprises—surprises that turn into beautiful memories for couples. These memories unite and strengthen the bond between partners. They are what make happy and successful couples. Every relationship has its unique memories. When these memories are combined with daily creativity, intimacy and tolerance increase significantly. This is not just a dream but a reality for couples who know how to cherish the best moments in their lives. Be one of them, and you will grow and shine like a star in the darkest city.

Your life is enriched when you embrace learning. Being in a relationship means creating more memories with your beloved spouse. You need to put in committed efforts; that is your home—a home of peace and enduring love. This journey will remind you of various memories that inspire you to strengthen your marriage. Do not lose hope; your spouse is your number one partner in cultivating those memories.

Hold each other's hands as you read this transformative book. Reflect on how you've managed to overcome tough and hurtful situations in your love life.

The Missing Moments

Do you remember how she missed you when you were away for a few months for work? Is this just a memory now? Love involves times when you have to miss the person you love. Work, studies, or business may physically separate you. However, do not let this distance become mental. Every couple goes through this stage. It's a time when temptations arise, and you might start to feel that someone close to you is more important than your spouse. If you're not careful, you might find yourself drawn to someone else while still married.

When life takes you through this season, pray and hold onto your faith. Continue loving your spouse despite the physical distance. Call or text him or her to stay connected mentally. Use this time to learn and strengthen your marriage. Avoid temporary distractions. Create and cherish as many memories as you can. Remind each other of how you used to live, how you used to share stories late into the night. When you miss someone, find a sweet and healthy way to connect with your spouse. She or he is still your sweetheart. Learn and keep moving forward.

Kisses and Hugs

Is she still pretty to you? Hug and kiss your partner often. This should apply to your husband as well. Both of you need this in your lives. A new marriage has plenty of kisses, but as time goes on, this may seem less important. Do not neglect your marriage.

When you leave for work, kiss and hug her. It's that simple. This simple gesture increases intimacy daily. Do not be rigid about this. Spend time playing together as you did when you were first in love.

Have you seen other couples carrying each other on their backs or dancing publicly with smiles? Why doesn't that spirit live in your marriage? Why is it tough to do? Remember, marriage is a joyful place, not a cage. Try incorporating these gestures into your daily life, and you'll find joy as time goes on. That's how you create and learn from the best memories.

A kiss symbolizes trust and restores hope that your partner is still *"the one."* Do it often, not just on special occasions like weddings or holidays. Marriage has daily holidays. Enjoy each day with your loved one. You've fulfilled the dream of having a life partner; now restore your love with a positive attitude. Hugging is a memory, and kissing is another lesson.

The Quiet Zone

Marriage has its darker hours—a time when everyone is silent and angry. Don't deny it. You might have forced him to turn off the television, and now he's angry and doesn't want to talk. He might even refuse to eat dinner with you. Moments like these should not push you into revengeful behavior. He might be right in the moment. Don't fight to be the winner, as in marriage, you always find what is enough for each other. Understand your role, and restore the situation with hope and courage.

Quiet time can bring loneliness, anger, and jealousy. A happy person knows when to express love. This quality of love is crucial. Often, relationships end in depression or breakups during these dark, quiet times. What do you learn from such hard times? Is it a time for reconciliation? Let these moments become lessons for you and your spouse. Learn from them and strive not to repeat them. Continue to strengthen your marriage.

Cherishing the Past

Dear lovely couples, do you often take pictures? Do you write notes to each other? Are you surprised by these questions? Love is a beautiful experience on Earth. Many people cry when they lose loved ones. Marriage has its phases. Today you may be happy, and tomorrow you might face sadness. As you live with your spouse, create the best moments of your life. Time will come when life pushes you apart, and things get tough.

You might plan to send your child to high school, but your husband refuses without clear reasons. She might need money for a salon, and you didn't provide it, causing her to ignore you. You might plan a date, but she says she's too busy. Every time you undertake a new project together, it seems to push you apart. When these things happen, believe that this is a short season. It will pass, and new memories will be added to your love story. Trust the process and keep building your togetherness.

Just as tough times can separate couples, so can sweet and happy moments. This journey reminds you to create as many memories as possible with your beloved partner. Create your love album. Keep those notes and stickers. If you write stories to your partner, keep doing so. Do as many wonderful things as you can. Relationships grow stronger not only through quality time but also by cherishing the best memories that nurture both of you.

Memories keep you firm. They restore your commitment and remind you that you rely on each other. They show you how you have endured numerous challenges. Focus on this continuously.

Teach each other how to be heroes in love. When your spouse is building a foundation, help her carry as many stones as possible. Be united. Remember, *"Tough times never last."* Do not separate during these periods. It is always painful to part from someone you have cultivated a life of love with for years. Let your scars heal by trusting your spouse. Remind her of the best memories you've created. When life teaches you lessons, be ready to learn. Do not quit. Learn and live.

Living Within Your Limits

Loving your spouse means understanding his or her limits. Everyone has limitations that act as boundaries separating them from others, including your spouse. When these boundaries are crossed, anger often results. Now is the time to understand these limits in your marriage. Set a day, whether at home or away, to discuss these boundaries. Let your spouse explain his or her limits, and listen while taking notes. Once they finish, share your own boundaries as well. This is how you start to understand each other's likes and dislikes.

Another task in marriage is to continually learn and adapt to updated limits. Life changes, as does your partner. His or her likes and dislikes evolve over time. Be his or her closest confidant. Have you seen couples wearing matching t-shirts? They look like beautiful flowers together. Whether young or old, they stick together in various places. This isn't just love; it's great support from your partner. Be that team. Fulfill this dream with your supportive spouse. Understanding limits will keep you safe and protected.

Take Home Love Message

Be united through your memories. Let them be the icons that daily unite you in your marriage.

"Two are better than one, because they have good reward for their toil. For if they fall, one will lift up his fellow. But woe to him who is alone when he fails and has not another to lift him up!" **Ecclesiastes 4:9-10.**

Getting Old

When you think you've exhausted all possibilities for nurturing your marriage in a positive way, remember this: you haven't. Love is meant to last. It requires endurance, commitment, and constant renewal. That journey begins and ends with you. Your marriage is your home—the life journey you chose when you made that covenant.

It's essential to review your principles and come back stronger. Focus on growing old not just in age but in love and wisdom. Dream big and make the most of your unique relationship. Learn from and cherish your partner. Years may come and go, but your commitment to that person remains the same. You will encounter failures, regrets, misunderstandings, and moments of doubt. These challenges are part of the love journey. There will be days when you feel like the person you married isn't right for you, or that you made a grave mistake that will enslave you until you die. It can feel like a prison without chains, filled with daily blame. When neither of you is willing to learn and unlearn your old ways, love suffers.

Love needs mutual understanding and daily peace. These are the key nutrients that feed a marriage. It's time to analyze what's preventing you from being the happy person you once were. Identify what is stopping you from growing old in love and discover what is undermining your marriage. If it's a new lifestyle, be ready to change. Marriage needs peace to grow, and you must be that peace.

What is Preventing You from Growing Old Together?

Love is like a patient admitted to the hospital; if you don't check on and care for her, she will deteriorate over time. Your time is now. Update your marriage with new ideas, fresh hope, and valuable lessons. Today, write down what's preventing you from growing old with that beautiful love of yours. Make a checklist and be ready for change. Don't hide any details.

Consider these questions: Is your marriage filled with jealousy, anger, a lack of forgiveness, selfishness, or feelings of superiority or inferiority? Why do you quarrel every day?

- Are you ready for change?

- Are you ready to learn and grow?

- What can you do to improve your relationship and your marriage?

- Do you want to enjoy love for the rest of your life with that wonderful husband?

It's time to renew your commitment. It's time to revisit the covenant. By doing so, you'll overcome many obstacles in your marriage. Regularly review your checklist and the questions you've asked yourself. Find new ways to restore happiness. Dream big and live it right now. Focus on yourself, your marriage, and your relationship. No one can make you happy if you don't change your perspective.

Break the chains that hold back your love. Break your loneliness. Promise yourself that you won't make the same mistakes again. Address the tough times—if it's ego, resolve it with respect and understanding. If there's a lack of spiritual connection, welcome it through fasting and praying together. Find positive solutions to each item on your checklist. Don't let a day, week, or month go by without finding a working solution to your problems. Hold hands as you navigate these challenges. Be a united front.

Become a Billionaire of Success

How old is your relationship? Is your love filled with success? Being in a marriage is a daily success. Happiness is a choice, and it's one you must make every day. Let your successes strengthen your marriage. Live according to your mission and vision.

Focus on one woman, and you'll be a billionaire of success. That woman should be your wife, and the same rule applies to husbands.

Success requires active planning. Sit down with your wife and make plans together. Don't be shy or nervous—everyone needs new lessons. Be her number one lesson and make her believe in you. Support her emotions, and success will always be your home. Success isn't an emergency; it's the result of hard work that transforms dreams into reality. Be together, live together, and grow old together.

One old man said, *"I am a successful man on Earth not only because of my principles but also because of the great support I receive daily from my beautiful wife. Whatever I do, she supports me. Whatever I think, she motivates me. Our love has grown old because we know when to celebrate and when to plan for the future. I always put new ideas into her mind. When I'm down, she comforts me. This is our motto: my success is hers, and her success is mine. I remind you, my son, focus on one woman, and you will enjoy daily success that God gives you through your wife. Don't forget that!"*

Be Home Rule

Home is peace. Home is love. Home is togetherness. Do you believe that? Being at home should have a proper meaning and a positive effect not only on your wife but also on your children. Make the people you love understand the meaning of home.

Be a positive force at home. When you're at home, let your woman enjoy your presence fully. Let her understand your purpose. Make this your daily routine. It increases trust, loyalty, and togetherness and brings peace to your spouse.

What do you do when you're at home? Does your spouse enjoy your presence? What about your children? Train yourself to be present at home. Your presence should have a daily positive impact. Invest in that. That's your peace. It's another way of learning the language of love.

Being *"home rule"* will help you understand what your spouse enjoys most when you're together at home. Free yourself from work and studies, and enjoy your free time with your family. Turn on the television and watch together as you did when you were young in love. Make dinner and sit together in the dining room with your beautiful wife. Teach her to understand what you're doing in the moment.

On special days like Valentine's Day, Christmas, Eid, and Easter, set a table at home and talk about your life. Assess yourselves each year. Remind each other when necessary. Love is shared at home. Love is your family, and that family begins with your spouse. Dear men, love begins at home.

Go to work, but don't forget your quality time with your wife. If things go wrong at your workplace, you may lose the comfort and support of your colleagues, but if you properly invest in your marriage, you will receive daily hope from your spouse. Never underestimate this rule. Be at home. Be a home for your partner.

Breakup Isn't Final in Marriage

A journey that is meant to last should always be cherished. Problems in your relationship are part of learning new ways of loving and enduring. No marriage is without challenges; they are part of life. What you need to do is learn from them and move forward. Problems can be overcome with faith and forgiveness. They are steps toward the restoration of love and peace in your marriage. Pray and plan your life of love with courage. Pray to God that you may never become a source of your marriage's downfall. Pray that you may not anger your partner to the point where his or her love diminishes forever, as that could kill your marriage and lead to a breakup. But don't just pray—make an active plan. Strengthen the pillars of your marriage. Don't sit back. Do it now.

Invest your energy into building strong pillars for your marriage. Make it a priority to listen to each other every time something goes wrong. Take time to resolve misunderstandings as they arise. He or she is a special person to you. Move from being just someone you know to a girlfriend, then a fiancée, to your wife, and ultimately to the mother of your children—an icon of your next generation. Do not aim to break your covenant. No one is perfect. No one is always right. In marriage, you both have enough for each other.

Breakup isn't final. Cherish your love. Cherish your marriage. Let your love live forever. You are the one to decide—decide what is best for your marriage. Don't add stress to your marriage. Fill it with peace, forgiveness, transparency, togetherness, accountability, and positive endurance. Don't sink your love ship. The journey continues, and you are the captain.

Adventures Will Heal Your Marriage

How do you spend your holidays? Have you ever planned a special place to visit this December? Do you think this could be a miracle for your marriage? Go to beautiful places, not alone but with your spouse. Go for walks. Go with your spouse. Prepare a picnic. Love isn't as serious as you might think. Stop taking things too personally. It's time to set your adventure plan. It's time to relax and go for a hike. Find time to swim and travel this Earth. You'll enjoy the view, create new memories, and strengthen your marriage.

Adventures will remind you of the golden gift hidden in your partner. Don't be naïve—find that place and enjoy the experience together. Don't forget your best camera. Don't worry about carrying all the luggage for your wife on a day or week trip. Today is the best day to laugh, to have fun with that beautiful partner. Free yourself from work, business, and other personal pursuits. It's time to engage in that special business with your spouse—and that business is adventuring with your soulmate.

Release your stress and feelings. Adventure requires a peaceful and open mind—a mind ready to meditate. Set your date. Set your place. If it's Christmas, fulfill that. If it's Easter, be together and enjoy it. Find a hotel, beach, or hiking spot and cuddle a lot. Don't forget to order a special dish that will create a memorable moment with meaning for your love. Eat together while laughing and smiling. Don't be too serious with each other like you're in an army parade waiting for orders from a captain. Love is a beautiful thing.

When on an adventure, plan how you'll move from where you are to the next bigger step. Plan how you'll correct past mistakes that have hindered your marriage. Plan how you'll last forever, positively. Concentrate on each other. Let each other understand that purpose. That is your love. That is your relationship. That is how you update your marriage with positive lessons. Enjoy your love. Enjoy your adventure and your growth in marriage. Will this be difficult to do in your marriage?

Old People Love Memories

How old are you in your marriage? How many memories have you created? Do you enjoy recalling those moments? Love is full of memories—from the day you first approached each other to the life you're living now. You should always create as many positive memories as possible to continue nurturing your marriage and love, regardless of your age.

Old people love memories, as do old couples. They have been through many lessons in life. As a couple, your marriage should be filled with sweet, life-changing moments. One day, go and visit your grandparents. Ask them how they overcame life's challenges to reach old age. Ask them about their marriage in today's world. Listen carefully to their stories. Don't rush to comment—aim to learn. You'll be amazed at how they'll show you their albums filled with pictures from different seasons.

Their memories are captured in a single album, and when you look at it, she'll explain everything in detail.

This is love—a love of memories. A love that has been planted, cultivated, irrigated, and cared for until old age. Dear couple, your love is made to last, not just in your youth but also into old age. You will pass through various seasons. Sometimes you'll quarrel; other times you'll laugh and smile. But don't forget to keep good memories. Don't forget to take pictures when you have the best smile of the season. Aim to be that kind of couple. Your time is now. Your old age is prepared by your current love life.

Live long enough to get old, and you will be among those who cherish memories. This will not only give you peace but will also continue to strengthen and teach other couples in love. Your memories will be the best lesson for everyone who watches you. Why not become such a partner? Don't forsake your old spouse. Don't make her sad. She still needs you. She still needs to learn something new. Your time is her quality time. Be together. Enjoy your marriage. Enjoy your old love. Learn from your positive memories.

Take Home Love Message

Love each other despite your current age. Live a love that lasts not only in your youth but also into your old age.

"Don't forsake me now when my strength is falling." **Psalm 71:9.**

To End is to Begin...

The Timetable That Will Always Save and Serve Your Marriage

Do you love your spouse? It's time to set your own timetable that will always remind you of what's best to do for each other. I know you have enjoyed reading this book from the beginning to this point. I know you value your spouse a lot. But love needs a guideline to nourish and flourish. You are the one to prepare your own guideline. Now, take a pen and a fresh piece of paper, and follow this lead:

• Choose a positive book about marriage and read it together for at least 20 to 30 minutes a day. You can do this at night or whenever you have free time together at home. Teach each other what you've learned from the reading. What book will you choose today?

• Take 5 to 10 minutes a day to pray together. Dear couple, this is a must. You must do it. I know it may be a bit difficult at first, but try to do as little as you can. The magic of prayer will enlighten your marriage. Pray every day, whether in person or over the phone.

• Make sure you eat together. No matter how busy you are, one of your three daily meals should be eaten at home with your spouse. Invest in this habit. Let it become part of your routine.

• Set aside time for enjoyment at least twice a week. You could watch TV, play games, or do anything fun for both of you. Make this a regular part of your routine.

• Physical fitness is crucial in your marriage. Include it in your timetable. Set a time to do physical exercises together. This doesn't just help maintain your shape; it also keeps you close to each other and supports your health. It strengthens your bond.

• Love needs a change of environment. Go for walks. Go outside your home. Plan special dates for picnics, sleepovers, or hikes. Change your environment and invest in your smiles. Start saving money for this purpose.

• Set a date for meditation and reconciliation. This is very important to remind you of the best things you can do for your spouse. Meditate often.

• Plan your weekly or monthly timetable and share it with each other. This will be a guideline for what you're going to do.

Your timetable will serve as a constitution to guide your married life. It will always remind you of what you need to do for each other. Through this, you'll always find quality time together despite your daily challenges. Write your timetable now, and remember to shuffle it so that you don't become too accustomed to it. Will you do that?

The Song of Forever Love Endurance

Hello, my love. I always understand your love.
I still remember the first day we met,
It was along the river,
But your first impression captured my heart,
Your voice conquered my mind,
Your smile made me laugh like a child.

You mean a lot in my life.
Your time is always exceptional,
Your care is always extraordinary,
You teach, and I always learn from you,
Together we quarrel, together we move on.

Our vow on the altar made us perfect,
Our commitment was written on paper,
Everyone was smiling and celebrating,
Tears became our "Yes" to each other,
Joy was the only language at the time.

Our journey isn't always special,
Sometimes we fight and fall silent,
But we hold each other's hands.
We give ourselves hope,
That tomorrow will be another beautiful day.

Our promise before marriage was strong,
We live together despite our differences,
We will stay together from youth to old age,
We will overcome whatever comes our way.

Love is a beautiful gift on Earth,
Do not discourage my love,
Protect my love like a queen,
Never leave me alone, my king,
Our marriage is our kingdom.

Cherish what is best for us.
Our love story is made to last.
Let's finish it together,
I love you. I believe in you,
I believe in your efforts,
I believe in our strong marriage.

The Positive Love Assessment Tool for Your Marriage

Have you sung that song of forever love endurance? A good marriage is one that has a positive assessment of where it came from, where it is, and where it wants to be. This is the kind of marriage that will last from youth to old age.

Use this score chart to assess your relationship. Aim to learn and correct where you have stumbled so that your married life will be filled with hope, perseverance, and positive endurance. Change your life by conducting regular monthly assessments.

S/N	Assessment	Response (Y for Yes and N for No)		Response percentage (%)	What is missing from you?
		Y	N		
1	Do you spend quality time with your spouse?				
2	Does your relationship have positive and effective communication?				
3	Are you able to easily read and understand your spouse's emotions and feelings?				
4	Is there creativity in your marriage?				

S/N	Assessment	Response (Y for Yes and N for No)		Response percentage (%)	What is missing from you?
		Y	N		
5	Is there patience within your marriage?				
6	Do you frequently teach each other new things about love?				
7	Is there forgiveness in your marriage?				
8	Do you often pray together?				
9	Do you regularly express gratitude to your spouse?				
10	Is there a sense of loneliness in your marriage?				
11	Does gift-giving characterize your marriage?				

S/N	Assessment	Response (Y for Yes and N for No)		Response percentage (%)	What is missing from you?
		Y	N		
12	Is anger a dominant factor in your relationship?	☐	☐		
13	How well do you comfort your spouse during tough times?	☐	☐		
14	Do you enjoy sex from your partner?	☐	☐		
15	Do you enjoy sexual intimacy with your partner??	☐	☐		
16	Do you always miss your spouse when you are apart?	☐	☐		

S/N	Assessment	Response (Y for Yes and N for No)		Response percentage (%)	What is missing from you?
		Y	N		
17	Does your partner understand your love language?				
18	Do you often feel protected when you are with your spouse?				
19	What kind of fear is undermining and harming your marriage?				
20	Are you planning to use this love checklist to enhance your marriage?				

Table 2: This love checklist will help you positively assess your marriage. Use it to improve areas where you have low scores and maintain consistency in areas where you score higher.

Let your marriage last longer by positively doing monthly and yearly assessments to see where you are and where you want to go together. Do this task individually, and let your partner do it as well. Compare your results and identify what's missing in your growing, God-gifted relationship. Your success begins with your positive commitment.

The Endless Love Endurance

The Proper Meaning of Your LOVE

You have to sort it out!

- **L** stands for *Learn and nurture your relationship and marriage through each stage of aging*. Understand that you are getting older; your feelings, responsibilities, outlook, and even your smile will change. How active and sexy you were in your youth will differ as you age. How you listen, multitask, order new birthday cards on time, remember important details for your spouse, and more will change. Learn to nurture the positive aspects and protect your marriage despite the ups and downs. Sort that out.

- **O** stands for *Obey your own love rules*. Each relationship has its rules, which act as guidelines to protect, direct, and restore what is best for you. If the rule is to be home by 7:00 pm, then be there. If it's to say sorry, make sure you do it often. If it's time to pray, take the best suit and hold her hand as you go to morning prayers—even indoor prayers work wonders. Obedience will strengthen your marriage despite your growth.

• **V** stands for *Verify your feelings for each other*. Sometimes it's hard to show how you feel, but remember that showing your feelings to your spouse is the best medicine for your love. Your spouse is your number one friend. Verify your feelings so he or she can help you. If you're sad, show it. If you're angry, show it. If you feel different from how you usually are, express it all. That's how they learn about you in a new, updated way. It hurts, but you have to relax your muscles for the injection to penetrate deeply.

• **E** stands for *Experience and explore more*. Now, you know him or her more than anyone. Yes, that's it. Your life is his or her experience, same as yours. You've been exploring each other for years, witnessing both good and bad things. Keep his or her secrets to yourself and continue exploring them positively. Don't let others know your marriage's deep problems. More beautiful and blessed years are waiting for you. Get old together and forever.

That's the proper meaning of your **LOVE**. Will you live this way?

Enjoy Your Life-Long Love Partnership

It's time to enjoy your journey, re-evaluate yourself and your marriage, and conclude what you've learned from your youth to old age. You're not truly wise if you only read to finish the pages of this life-changing book. Review your marriage and be ready to transform, meditate, correct, and maintain that forever love happiness. Fulfill all the goals you've set. Work as a team.

Love is like a growing tree. It grows from a seed to a fully matured tree with fruits to feed birds and other animals. This is your love. Allow yourself to learn and relearn while going through tough situations. Don't break your partnership when tough times become your temporary companion. Use this book to revive your commitment and move toward endurance.

Consider your relationship as your number one paying job. Don't allow yourself to be seduced by other temporary jobs that have no value. Focus on one job and achieve your visions. As time passes, you'll get older. The time will come when you'll lose all qualifications of being an employee. If you don't prepare yourself, you'll regret not taking the right decisions. Think with hope and invest in your spouse as you continue getting older in love.

Give thanks to each other for the best decision you've made so far—the decision that has made you one of the world's successful couples. Say thanks to your handsome husband while finishing the last page of this book. Promise yourself that you will not leave each other in hard times. Respect and invest in nurturing your marriage. Your success is determined by your daily commitment. It's never too late to learn what's best for your marriage.

Dear couple, you need to read and re-read this book. Score yourself each year to see if your love is getting better. Live with a person who understands your values—someone who knows how to invest not only in your youth or adulthood but also in your old age. He or she knows the right time to harvest in each season. That's the spouse you should live with. And that spouse should be yourself and not anyone else. The journey of forever love endurance begins with changing yourself. Dream and live it right now. Believe in yourself. Believe in your marriage.

Other Books written By Dr. Stanlaus Luwanda

1. Another side of LoVE – *Moving togethe*r

2. Muda na Wazazi – *Mwepesi wa Kujifunza*

3. The Change – *Overcoming Tough Times with Positive Mindset*

To get hard copies of each book contact the author via Phone number +255 786 334 448.

Be inspired with Dr. Stanlaus Luwanda by His daily teachings, inspirations and wisdom through social medias at;

Instagram: stanluwanda

Facebook: stanluwanda

Twitter: stanluwanda

Thread: stanluwanda

Email: stanlaus@outlook.com

Website: stanthechange.mailerpage.io

For personal development seminars & programs contact Him via Phone number: +255 786 334 448 or check him at stanlaus@outlook.com

Protect your love, protect your kingdom, protect your marriage.

ABOUT THE AUTHOR

Dr. Stanlaus Dimosso Luwanda (MD) is a medical doctor who earned his degree from Kilimanjaro Christian Medical University College (KCMUCo) in Moshi, Tanzania, in 2020. He currently works as a general practitioner in Kongwa District, Dodoma, Tanzania.

In addition to his medical career, Dr. Luwanda is a motivational and public speaker, as well as a counselor specializing in personal development, health, relationships, and marriage. He is a coach dedicated to fostering positive life changes.

Dr. Luwanda is also the author of three books: **MUDA NA WAZAZI, ANOTHER SIDE OF LOVE,** and **THE CHANG**E. His inspirational works have positively transformed the lives of many readers. He also conducts seminars for individuals and organizations on topics such as planning, development, and human discipline.

Dr. Luwanda is married to his best friend, Dr. Marina Martin. He believes, *"Love is the source of all your positive, hardworking plans for your marriage. Nurture and live your marriage love now and often."* His life philosophy is centered on planning and discipline: *"Discipline yourself and your marriage. Be inspired by your positively planned life."*

END.

FROM YOUTH TO OLD AGE

A Love Journey of Forever Endurance

A Love to last is a marriage to endure.

The journey of a successful & committed marriage begins by understanding your spouse's true potential in your love life. Your beginnings, your dreams, your investment and your memories are going to be a life time transformational ladder towards growth and lasting.

In this book, you are going to last **FROM YOUTH TO OLD AGE** in your marriage love by going through the ten strong & positive life changing journey in nurturing your relationship. Your intimacy, your quality time, your inspirational love, and your parenthood love are going to boost your morale towards positive endurance. It's time to love, learn, care and lead your marriage love to old age.

Dr. Stanlaus Luwanda is a medical doctor, counsellor, speaker, life coach and an author of four books. He also provides personal development seminars concerning planning & discipline.

He is a 2020 medical graduate from Kilimanjaro Christian Medical University College (KCMUCo) – Moshi, Tanzania. Invest & protect your marriage. Life is planning and discipline.

Stay in touch with Dr. Stanlaus Luwanda for daily teachings, programs and inspirations at; stanlaus@outlook.com and stanthechange.mailerpage.io

ISBN 978-9912-42-091-5

 @stanluwanda